UX/UI
FOR
LEAN STARTUPS

A Guide to Researching Practical Techniques for Designing Unique User Experience and Better Products

MAURICE
JAYSON

Copyright

Maurice Jayson
ISBN: 9798675964901
ChurchGate Publishing House
USA | UK | Canada
© Churchgate Publishing House 2020

Printed in the United States of America
© 2020 by Maurice Jayson

Contents

CHAPTER ONE

INTRODUCTION TO UX DESIGN

To the uniformed mind, getting to understand the nitty-gritty of UX design is more like rocket science. To them, why should they care about what people feel about their products? After all their products are only available to just some few people. If you care to ask, people with this kind of mentality rarely succeed in online business. Emotion is at the core of human feelings, and people most likely tend to go for a product which gives them maximum satisfaction.

The UX design means User experience design and it revolves around designing an ideal user experience for your products. When you are keen about getting feedback for your products, and you are in the process of designing a system where your customers are able to tell you how they feel about your product; then you are considering a User experience design. Generally, the User experience design is a mostly used term when you are talking about web applications, software applications and websites designed to cater for people's ultimate needs. It is okay to say that User experience design might be a time consuming and demanding endeavor for the little minded, such that if you are not worth your salt; you would probably consider not getting started at all. The User experience borders on a lot of topics and concepts designed to get you initiated into the system. Whether you are an entrepreneur trying to launch your new product or you are just a web developer who is keen on getting feedback about his website usability, the field of UX design comes loaded with a lot of things you can lay your hands on to get the job done for you. The User experience design has created jobs for teeming majority of active individuals who take it their job to provide a unique User experience design process for business owners or other persons who just want to take their products to the next step and make more money.

If you are a student of history, or someone who enjoys relating the past with the present; you would most willingly agree that the websites we have online now are content richer than what was obtainable some decades ago. The reason is not far fetched as websites users can now, unlike before, relate their experience using a website or a product on the website to the developer who will in turn improve on the user experience. You can incorporate website features from Mars or order more improved website plugins from Jupiter, the success of your website or products still depend on consumers' feedback.

UX designers are mostly concern with the following basic questions about their products or website;

- **Is the product or the application providing the necessary value to the consumer:** Most times, you might think you are giving the end users the exact thing they need; but this might not be so. Asking yourself this simple question will go a long way toward giving you the necessary approval and validation about your project or product you are giving the public.

- **Is the website or the product user-friendly?** The product or website must not be one to give users a tough time to use or navigate. If the product needs an instruction manual, endeavor to include one that is easy to read for the user.

- **Are the consumers enjoying the product or the website?** While it is easy to gauge, judging from your own perception, the user preference for your product, it won't be a good idea to conclude or assume that users admire your product or website. One good index you can deploy to gauge this is if your website is getting attention from a diverse group of people who find your services interesting or worth their time. A good UX design can help you to understand how well users are enjoying your products. This can be accomplished by putting a platform or system where users can actually get to talk to you about your products and the immense benefit they are getting from your services.

If you can tick yes to all the three simple questions above, then you can be sure your product is doing a nice job which is a good sign.

In summary, user experience is literally how users feel when they utilize a particular product or service. In most instances, the product we are referring to will be an application or a website of some sort. Every case of human-object relationship has an associated user experience linked with it, but, in most cases, UX designers are concerned with the connection between human consumers and computers and computer-based products, such as applications, systems and websites.

A UX designer is a person who is interested in the investigation and analysis of how consumers feel about the products they are using. The UX designer can be the product's manufacturer or literally someone who has been employed by the product maker to help design a UX platform for a product. The UX designer collects all the information and consumers' perception about a product to further improve the product and give consumers the best product experience they desire. UX designers are researchers and analysts and are in the best position to tell other parties in the development team about their findings. UX designers follow project development to make sure their research is properly documented and utilized in the design of the final product.

Why UX? Does it really matter?

In the days of old, product innovators and designers make products they think will attract users' attention and will give them maximum satisfaction. Notice the use of the word "**think**" Yes! Those days, once a manufacturer feels a product is good, he will invest in the product and start selling such product to the users. This approach worked then because there was no stiff competition for online marketing, as few people actually understand the processes of bringing their products online. Today, technology has brought the needed change to the internet, and now, unlike before, people are getting access to ideas they can use to market their products or websites online. This translates to stiff competition, hence your product must be one giving people the needed satisfaction, otherwise they will move to your competitor. Implementing a UX design for your product ensures that your product is tailor made for the consumer, and you can avoid producing a product just because you think people will like it.

Project environment where UX designs can be found

It is worthy to reiterate that not every business or startup will require a UX design. Most companies or organizations that usually employ UX ideas are those businesses who want to take the game to the next level without compromising on quality. There are some factors which can hinder an organization capability of implementing UX designs in most of their tasks. Factors such as budget and industry's size have a very long way to determine an organization's need for a UX designer. Nonetheless, the following projects are projects where you most probably would need the service of a UX design;

- **Long term projects:** projects can be a short term project or a long term project. A long term project takes a long time for completion, and you can't underestimate the importance of having a UX plan for such a project. Having a UX plan for a long term project will enable you to gauge your progress at every point of the project's process. This will ensure you come out with a product, which is not only user-friendly but also tailored to meet users' demand.

- **Startups companies or businesses:** Although, most startups nowadays don't feel the need of having a UX design as part of their design processes, but startups who want to get their products across regions should consider a UX design process. Startups dealing in high-tech need to understand that an efficient user experience design interface will actually be useful to get a clue of what consumers feel about their products. This is so that they can improve on their software or products or applications going forward. Let us for example assume that you just open a startup company who is into building and designing video game applications. You released the video game out so that users can start enjoying the games at their convenience. You can implement a User experience design system

6

that will help you manage and collect data of how users feel about your game.

- **Projects that include a lot of money:** While small projects might not really have much when it comes to finance, big projects should be able to dedicate a decent part of their budget to UX.
- **Complicated projects:** Some projects are actually more complicated than another. The more difficult the project at hand, the more required the UX design. Say for instance, Samsung released a device called Samsung Note 20 Ultra, the only way the Samsung company can get to know if any part of their gadget design is not working effectively is through User experience design.

UX Design processes and documentation

Documentation at every stage is the face of UX. When you want to visualize, create and measure a product's performance, you would need a documentation process for proper assessment of all the processes involved in the design stage. Kindly understand that project design and documentation is not at all the same across all organizations. You cannot expect to have the same product design and documentation when you are making a car product with another company producing phone gadgets. Nonetheless, you can find the overview below a useful guide to understand the process of proper documentation irrespective of the niche of your organization. These documentation strategies actually work and you can, in fact, adapt the ones you think will suit your organization's and product's requirements.

Most people are always theoretical with zero practical. When you want to be successful with product design document-ation, you need to learn how to balance theory with actions. Every part of the documentation process must synchronize with a unique research methodology, proto-typing, and also the documentation stage. One important question people ask most often is how they can relate all of the processes involved in documentation together to create a single framework from which all the system will be taking a clue from. It all actually boils down to enabling docum-entation in your design process just to complement your already existing protocols and rather not a supplement to your design process. But before anything else, let us actively take a look of documentation processes during product building. The guide below will show you how each step of the design documentation actually works together to achieve the best output.

1. First thing first, that is the idea here. The initial process of product definition involves, most usually, a group of stakeholders and innovators coming together to deliberate on the methodologies to adopt in order to have a successful project completion. During such deliberation,

action plans are often agreed on what the project is all about bordering essentially on concept maps and overview of what the company is trying to build or invest in.

2. Getting your hands dirty with research. This stage is where your team sits down to dot all I's and cross all T's. This stage might be a little demanding depending on the project's resources, amount of existing knowledge your team has about the product or project at hand, project's complexity and a host of other necessary factors which depend on the type of project you want to execute. Essentially, it is best to map out market analyses and carry out a customer review to determine what sells best and what consumers will like to buy and how they want it. In a case where you even have an existing product or business, it is essential you do a thorough review of the product. This is necessary to gauge if that product is still in demand or is one that will attract the attention of users.

3. During the **analysis** stage, all the product marketing data you must have collected so far will open the door for personas, documents you will need for each stage and the needed experience. At this stage, the definition of your product, what the product will actually prioritize and the plan necessary to actualize your products must have been thoroughly mapped out and should be available for formal design deliverables. You should endeavor to have more diagrams and sketches at this stage as they help refine

your thought while providing the door you would need to navigate to actualize each product's development.

4. You can create a mockup plan, active scenarios, and concept maps from the result you get in step 3 above. This will bring you straight into the **design stage.** Some formal documentation you can think about in this phase includes prototypes, wireframes, task-flow drawings, products sketches and design specifications. For instance, the personas data you collected and the competitive analysis during the research stage will be deployed into the intermediate and high level deliverables like the story-boards, wireframe and detailed mockup plans. Most companies pack the design stage and the research analysis as one large stage to achieve an overall effective strategy for the design process.

5. During the implementation stage, code and design assets will be assembled to build a product that complies with the product design specifications.

6. After the launching of the final product comes the real user experience design. In this stage, the product has been released for use and what is next is the feedback from the users who have been enjoying the product one way or another. Feedback systems such as bug reports, support tickets, product compliance etc should be implemented to refine the product through necessary upgrading and product iterations. Your company should endeavor to

monitor these product data generated in the form of analytics just to further successful deployment of the product.

7. Non-stop, data-driven product refinement is achievable by measuring and then iterating the steps from production to delivery, using the performance dashboards and analytics.

Principles to move your product to the next stage

Having understood how all the stages involved in the documentation process are linked together, it is time, now, to see how you can move your product along each stage of the documentation process. It might be important to understand how to use a design sprint to proffer solutions to your design problems. Three most important determinants for design sprint are **team's collaboration, reduced handover friction and** also the team focus. It is safe to say that your documentation must be a unique collaborative attempt that should delve and take care of the uses themselves. When you navigate between each step of the documentation process, you will be able to gain standing momentum and can always reduce waste. More importantly, you're tackling smaller problems which allows for more exploration and risk-taking.

The guide below will take you through the necessary things needed to understand the product you want to build, create or design your product and then release the product for the end-users while not compromising on the product improvement designs.

1. UNDERSTANDING THE PRODUCT

Before you can create your product, you will need to understand why the product must exist in the first place. What specific problem will your problem solve? Is your product going to be a source of job creation or will be one that will rob people of their job? Is your product harmful or toxic to both lives and the environment? All these questions must be properly addressed before you can convince a potential investor to invest in your project development. You might be required to add actions that buttress end-user requirements, excellent design strategies and the business requirement. Your business activities must be strong and defendable enough to attract the attention of interested stakeholders, if not, you would only be convincing some bunch of people who already know why and how your actions and business plan will not work. If you have a good project to execute, and you would need the help of a collaborator or an investor, you can consider the following tricks;

• Having a stakeholder interview — You can dedicate some members of your team to interview at least three (3) stakeholders. The questions you can ask the stakeholders should border around the following contexts;

- How do stakeholders think the product will make the consumer feel: don't forget that stakeholders are humans too with feelings. They, most likely, will be part of the product user. Asking them questions about how they think the product will make them feel will go a long way to gauge your consumer preferences.
- What will the customer do if the product is satisfactory or not satisfactory? The stakeholders will willingly tell you some ideas and unbiased opinions, that you would most likely be biased about when you ask yourself. By taking note of how stakeholders think product consumers will feel about the product, you are setting a gauge to compare against user analysis and product's usability testing.

• Requirements workshops — Call a meeting of stakeholders, talk about the plans you have for the project at hand and delve more into the technical requirement of the product.

• Go numbers — Take your pen, pencil or markers and ask every member of your team to draw up about six, seven or eight product ideas within six, seven to eight minutes maximum. Tell all the members to score these products ideas. By doing so, you will get to know about individual preferences and what tickles humans at the most basic level.

As soon as you have successfully laid out all the initial work, you can begin to talk to and test your products with a wide number of users. This will give you accurate field data which you can deploy for your research and analysis. You can collect verified users' preferences and opinions, and utilize their ideas and insights to build your personas, create many amazing user stories and then map out the product requirement. Getting users' opinion gives the product team ample chance to work on the product much more to appeal to the taste and demand of the end-users.

2. THE PRODUCT DESIGN

You can't design a product without having, first, a sense or an idea of what purpose the product will serve. Your first thought about project design should be to build the project's prototype. The prototype is not the actual product; the prototype merely represents how you want the final product to look like. Get your team members to work so that you can eventually come up with something nice and presentable. One unique thing about this stage is that the documentation stage is the large chunk of the design for most of the deliverables. No matter which prototyping method you adopted, be sure to try it out with users and relevant stakeholders. For an all-round experience and design process, you can make a product map that will highlight and predict where and how the product has failed users' tests. While these are not necess-arily part of your product design process, they can be regarded as complementary because you are entitled to know whether your product fits into users' mind and is market worthy.

3. BUILDING AND LAUNCHING YOUR PRODUCT

As you begin to get started with the product's heavy technical requirement, it is best to have documentation which will help you to get the overall vision. Certain product requirements may change during the product's refining stage, but the documentation will help you to understand what to prioritize and what should be left for later steps. You can, in fact, imagine the product requirements and those technical specification documents as a roadmap to get things done for you. The product road map will show user stories and allow you to prioritize those product features you will include to satisfy your consumers. You can sometimes include dates inside the roadmap to serve as a timeline for achieving your desired objectives. The beauty of the roadmap is that it enables you to prioritize whichever product you want to create which serves as a complement to the product's "how" specified by the product requirements and technical needs. When you are in the process of deciding your product's features, you can utilize the Kano Model to outline and evaluate your product's features in three (3) categories:

• Product's Basic Attributes — These are the basic necessities that are essential for the product to function. For instance, a phone's basic attribute is the battery and screen.

• Product's Performance Attributes — You can use product's attributes to compare between two similar products or gadgets from different or the same manufacturers.

For instance, a laptop is primed on its CPU speed and the space on the hard drive since end-users usually admire fast computers that can keep lots of data.

• Delightful Attributes — These attributes are actually subjective and are a function of the customers' preferences. For instance, the Macbook Air is ultra thin and sleek to the touch. Some end-users would consider this a better selling point, while most others would not even be moved a bit. When you grade products on a scale of 1-5, you can plot it out using a prioritization matrix. This will enable you to imagine what the roadmap of your product will look like. When you take into notice all the responsibilities, various stages of product creation and all the noticeable milestones from product inception to the product launching stage, you are on the road to having an overall product plan worthy of documenting and shared with project investors and stakeholders.

4. MEASURING YOUR PERFORMANCE

After the building and eventual launching of your products, your documentation must as well borders on measuring and tracking sales success. Be reminded that you might not be able to improve your applications or products if you don't even understand the metrics and standards you want to adopt. To help you, you can enumerate your launch goals. For example, let us say you developed a video game application, your launch goal can be **"15,000 downloads in 15 days."** You must ensure that you possess the accurate systems and tools in place that can help you properly measure and document your progress.

You can utilize some metrics tools and software that can report bugs to initiate recurring reports to keep notice of your product's progress during the first few months of launching the product, and even beyond. You can also customize your product design and send your users custom surveys to know how you are doing with your product. You can utilize the current metrics and prioritization matrix to access the product's current benefit against the stress of improving its features to satisfy local consumption. If you notice that the effort is worth it, you can proceed to revamp and improve the product's features for local consumers' satisfaction.

Let Your Processes Be Objective

When you are mapping out your product design documentation, there is no one-fits-all approach. At the same time, you should understand that the product development stages and that of the user experience design are actually a subjective process, you should not endeavor to not let your documentation processes be a subjective process. When everything all boils down to normal, one of the main reasons your product is out there is to generate revenue directly or indirectly. There is nothing subjective about making money. You can go a very detailed documentation process or rather opt in for a light method, the end goal is about the same thing; getting your idea out of your head for people's consumption. Your documentation processes must not be a rigid one, but should rather serve as bearing for the final product. Most of the stages discussed above can be followed sequentially or you can modify them as you wish. Just make sure you are doing the right thing to get that idea live.

Defining your products before getting into the actual design

The Product Definition phase will go a long way toward determining whether your product will be massively successful or not. Failure to understand what this stage is all about might set the whole process to fail. When you are working to develop a product, two things you should steer far from are untested assumptions and unnecessary ambiguity as they most often lead to confusion and misunderstanding between team members. The first stage of product design mostly takes its energy from brainstorming about the products with expert team members and relevant stakeholders. The brainstorming, oftentimes, leads to project start off or some rough sketches, at the very least, of how the product or project will look like. The guide below will; set right on the path to understanding everything about the project or product defining stage.

Project definition? Does it even matter?

If you care to examine the definition of a product, you must have probably seen that a product is something that can be taken to a market, whether online or physical market, so that people who need it can have the right access to it; either for free or at a price. From this definition, one thing is obvious which is that a product is made for people's consumption. Many products, even, don't meet this simple qualification as the products are either unsatisfactory or don't even deserve to be called one.

A good product must be desirable, feasible and viable. When you walk into an Apple store to buy an iPhone, you are not only buying the iPhone; you are buying iPhone, prestige, cleanliness and customer reception that come with the device. To enable you have a good grasp of tangible products and intangible products, consider the product classes below;

• The Core Product — This is the satisfaction you get from buying a product. For example, the core product of your phone is making calls and receiving messages, not the phone itself.

• The Actual Product — This is literally what the end-user will call the physical (touch) product. It delivers the satisfaction you enjoy from the core product. Actual products can be indexed on few essential features such as brand, packaging, level, styling and levels.

• Augmented Product — This stands for some additional services and satisfactions you can associate with the actual product you purchased. You might be required to pay a premium service for the augmented product. The augmented product enables you to tailor the actual or core product based on the individual end-user. For instance, the IBM gadgets recorded their massive successes owing to their top-notch software and after sale services, and rather not due to the real product. In your project kick off stage, you need to map out why users will opt for your product and not that of a competitor.

The Kick-off Meeting

The kick-off meeting entails the advanced outline of the purpose for which the product is meant for, who is involved in the product's design and development, the approach they can use to work together as a team to monitor the product's progress and which success metric they are going to adopt. During the kick-off stage, a brief description of your product's documentation can be presented to the team and the collaborators at large by using a PowerPoint presentation. The following tips will guide you to have a good kick-off meeting;

1. PREPARING FOR THE KICK-OFF

The project kick-off is much the exact replica of a grand opening, bringing all the main players together in a moment to share ideas, information and a common purpose. You should endeavor to take proper advantage of this one-time opportunity to further energize the group, map out proper expectations, and set procedures needed to complete the project on time and within the approved budget. You can incorporate these four essential steps in your kick-off preparation to have a well rounded experience;

• Develop your project goals, aims and deliverables — Defining these essential items will enable you to decide on resourcing and planning for your product. What are the things that can interest the stakeholders in this project? Why are you making this project at this time and not another time?

• Identify your team members and responsibilities — Resources can vary depending on the size of the product and the complexity of the product. Ensure that you take into consideration what you need from the product design, development, support, marketing and operation team.

• Develop a rough plan of your product — Highlight all the risks and opportunities inherent in the product. This enables you to validate whether you possess the best resources and enables you to estimate the needed timelines for tasks and achievable milestones.

• Define key success factors — You need to be able to justify why the product you are developing is important to your company. In the same vein, metrics should be in place for you to be able to determine your success level. These success metrics must be appropriately communicated to the relevant stakeholders and team members who are working hands in hands to ensure the successful completion of the project at hand. When establishing communication with relevant stakeholders before the kick-off stage, it helps to break communication and ensures all intentions are properly communicated at the right time. You can, at this stage, even consider some hard questions for yourself. For instance, ask yourself what you can do to ensure the task at hand is actually a worthy investment. Allay their fears and let the stakeholders understand why the business is a success even before getting started. The stakeholder interviews will also help you to have a list of high-level functional requirements.

2. DOING THE KICK-OFF

Once you have completed all the necessary preparation, it is now time to gather up all your team members and all that you have understood about the project. In theory, the kick-off meeting you have with the relevant stakeholders should have many energy and amazing moments, and your team members should ingrain positivity that can leave the stakeholder amused and determined to help in your business.

Whether you are just getting started in business or product development, the success of a kick-off meeting is dependent on the amazing people and team members reviewing the plan with you.

3. GUIDING PRINCIPLES

Whether you are working on a kick-off or holding a kick-off meeting, having a set of guiding principles to follow will actually prevent you from going astray. You can consider the following tips;

• Concentrate your points very well — Research your points very well and make sure your meeting agenda centers around useful things.

• Have as many smart minds as possible around you during the kick-off process — It is best to have too many teams up front rather than getting to know in the end that you forgot to include a particular person who could have make the idea more successful.

• Build your meeting activities around "risk-free" exploration — Your kick-off process must be one that explores the ultimate potential for what is considered feasible, so endeavor to leave egos at the entrance.

• Bring fun and creativity — The meeting doesn't necessarily need to be boring. Bring jokes and laugh.

Concept Maps & Mockups

This is one useful way you can use to define the tangible and intangible part of your product. A concept map, more often than not, starts with a central idea or concept and then focuses to tell you how the central idea can be deciphered and broken down into simpler and specific concepts or topics. A concept map can be visualized as a structured idea that emphasizes a specific topic of interest involving collaboration between one or more team members. The end goal is to come up with a representation of how concepts and ideas can be interlinked to produce a desirable result. The following tips will guide you when you are in the process of making a concept map that works;

• Use easy to understand and non-coded language — The less ambiguous the language, the more easily you can be represented and understood. Use a good tone and focus only on the topic of interest.

• Iterate as much as possible — Start coming up with your concept map as soon as you start your product definition. Draw the map over and over both in your brain and on paper so that it sticks perfectly. With each iteration you carry out, you can get to know about more concepts and ideas that were not even in your initial plan before in the product definition phase and redraw frequently.

• Initiate a hierarchy — You can let a smaller part of your key concepts and ideas more visible, allowing team members and others to have a good grasp of the overall project structure and dive into detail when needed.

• Involve relevant stakeholders — The concept map derives its energy from healthy collaborations. You will need to energize your concept map by validating it with relevant stakeholders. This will ensure that your visions and goals are properly assessed and realigned to meet your target.

Concept maps improve understanding by displaying both the project and the goal in a single view. In addition to what has been said previously, you can as well create an idea mockup which will run as a check showing your project and product's overall structure. Essentially, concept maps can be regarded as a good foundation for product documentation.

Concept mockups can be used as initial explorations for your detailed mockups later, early sketches for your wireframes, and give visual representation for storyboards. Similar to a concept

maps, the concept mockups gives a unique avenue to reason differently, initiates a wide variety of ideas as quickly as possible and is often a low-risk method of navigating alternatives with relevant stakeholders.

Sketching out your concept map or a mockup is a quick method of experimenting with a variety of product ideas — and the bigger the project at hand, the more the ideas you would need to explain it and the more valuable your sketching will turn.

Defining Your Vision

This is 21st century and products have morphed beyond the item you can feel in your hands at any local shop. In fact, something as trivial as health insurance, the internet or an app made for dating can all be regarded as products in a true sense. This is because a product is essentially anything people buy to make their lives easy, and the items mentioned above all work to make things easier for people. Making a tangible or even an intangible product out of the blues needs an intuitive approach. As you navigate through the product definition step, you will in fact get to understand that the power of your product definition essentially depends on what you include as much as what you exclude.

When you think of all the ideas that are trekking around, you will realize that you might of course obtain more value from knowing what your product should not be.

As a follow-up, you can consider asking yourself the following basic questions; is your idea in sync with the vision of the organization you are working with? If No, try and re-strategize! Do you have another product option that can give more yields even with less time and financial investment? Do your ideas line up with the direction of the company?

A well assessed kick-off meeting, concept sketching and business canvases can provide justice to all these questions. This simple elimination strategy can enable you to prioritize goals and products while being mindful of poor product judgment. It is as well important to measure how consumers will feel about your product using some metrics, which have been previously discussed.

CHAPTER TWO

RESEARCHING YOUR PRODUCT BEFORE GETTING TO THE DESIGN STAGE

Product definition and product researching process are exactly interconnected. This is because there is no way you can get to define a product without even understanding why such a product exists in the first place. As soon as you are done with the product definition, the next thing on the agenda is to research about the product you have defined. Product research doesn't just happen inside your office or in your room; you go outside your domain to be able to consider diverse opinions as much as possible. The product research usually features the **market research** and **user research.** The product research can be imagined to be the other part of the building important to build a great product. The human mind is a complex machine, and what tickles Mr A at the basic level might not necessarily be the same thing that tickles Mr B at the same level. Needless is to say we all have individual tastes and preferences. To extend things the more, you are required to visualize consumers both as collective (focusing on what the majority like i.e market research) and individual (user research). Market research literally involves considering the larger part of the populace to understand what they are looking to see in a particular product, while user research, on the other hand focuses on sourcing information that satisfies individual tastes. Both the user research and the market research have a role to play in product innovation and can equally help drive new product ideas.

Product research? Why does it even Matters

In essence, knowing who you are creating the product for is as equally important as understanding the reason why you are making such a product. And if you don't understand why you are creating the product, then you should not be thinking about creating the product in the first place. Creating a product without considering the end user is a fast track route to product failure. Getting to see how all the pieces fit together is a holistic way to have a defined product tailored to meet consumer satisfaction.

If you don't have a product yet on the market, research tricks such as market segmentation and competitive profiling helps you to understand the necessary scale and profile of your investments. It is understandable that market research enables you to distinguish between the addressable market and distinguishable market:

• Total addressable market (TAM) — This represents the sum revenue opportunity for the product you created. It is safe to think of the TAM as the planet for your products.

• Serviceable available market (SAM) — This represents the part of the addressable market in which you can actually compete. It is safe to think of the SAM as the neighborhood for your products.

Understanding your available market is like half of a battle won, because at this point, you will get a clear idea of how to segment your customers and other neighborhood competitors. Research is good at giving guidance on designing solutions since it examines how a person utilizes a product — not data of what you think they are likely to buy. For example, your market research might identify that a favorable market exists for your product in Africa or an Asian country. But what is often profitable and what is much desirable might be two different things. The user research can now establish this assumption by telling you how people use other products against how they use your own products.

Market Segmentation Report

A market segmentation report is essentially a document that can examine your potential customers based on their individual and shared needs and preferences. Generally speaking, consumers are most often segmented by demographic, behaviors, psychology, benefits, geography or some mixture of these segregation factors. Your market report should identify three prime market bases which are; behavioral bases, descriptive bases and benefit bases. All of these benefit bases are part of customer traits which you need to consider moving your product forward. Check below the three lists of benefit bases and a little description about them;

• Descriptive bases — As the name implies, these talk about factors which describe demographics (gender, age, income, family size, etc) and geography (climate/population/region, etc).

• Behavioral bases — The behavioral bases are not easy to compute unlike the descriptive bases. They show a more powerful purchasing index. The behavioral bases explore the personal motivation which guide why buyers buy what they buy at each given time. Some of the motivations that guide consumer preferences include social class, brand loyalty, personality, lifestyle etc.

• Benefit bases — This segmentation approach is actually the most logical base and it assumes that segments exist to fulfill consumer benefits. One disadvantage, obviously, is that buyers are human and are not always logical or understand, sometimes, why they want the things they want. As such, you need to have a combination of benefit bases to depict reality. It is okay to add that strict segmentation can sometimes cause you to miss out on some consumers who are considered profitable (like adults who like adult contents or kids who like kid's content) when you focus your attention on a specific group within the populace. You can combine the segmentation report with your user research to let you get beyond what is ordinarily obtainable in theory.

Survey Results

Steve Jobs, the then Apple CEO once explained " it is not the consumers' job to understand what they want; for we know what they want before they even think they do and we give it to them." While this might be true, it is still in your best interest as a beginner to inquire what consumers want first through a survey analysis since you don't opine that the consumer should go ahead and design the product themselves.

Survey results can be imagined as a baseline index for your product. Though, they are not mandatory for all products' success. But any idea to see into what the consumers think is a welcome one. The survey conducted online can serve as a blueprint for a low-cost method that enables you to visualize patterns for your data very quickly.

Focus groups and interviews are other alternatives to online surveys. Though they are costly – because they involve looking for potential customers, preparing tailored questions and then pay people to interview – but they still provide a good way of analyzing and getting to understand consumers' preferences. But if your budget is not exactly robust, an online survey will still give you ample data to work with. If you have chosen the online survey method, you can consider the tips below for massive success;

• Have an achievable goal and understand how to get it: Be crystal clear with your goals, who do you want to address, and what do you wish to know? Try and make it short, this way you will be able to ask direct and straightforward questions you only need answers for. A five (5) survey, sometimes, can be more productive than a one hour (1 hour) survey which doesn't even center on the areas that need to be addressed.

• Put ideas to live on paper — put down every question you required answers to. You can have a list of 8 to 20 questions, rephrase these questions in a different approach and make sure they all center on the problem you want to solve.

• Edit all over again — Arrange your original list of questions into common themes and then select one out of each theme. Let us assume you only want 6 questions, if you have more than 6, you can start to edit these questions to arrive at what you want.

• Design your questions very well — there are two categories of questions that you can consider here; closed and open questions. While a closed question provides a restricted choice of answer to the person that wants to answer it, an open question allows consumers to freely express their thoughts and you can always learn as much as possible from such a scenario. The close-ended questions don't give room for free answers and only binary yes/No answer is allowed. But no matter what questioning method you opt for, it is important that you ask good questions that demand answers that can bring you, if not at the same level, very close to what the consumers want. You should also try as much as possible to make your questions short.

• Order your questions — Ordering questions appropriately actually matters. The most important questions should come first. If you want to follow up, you can ask your questions last (if you ask them at the beginning, people will ignore you because they don't know you).

If your budget is robust enough, it is advisable you standardize your questions and then find the right people who are knowledgeable enough to provide the right answer to your questions without bias. You need to be selective when you consider the open-ended question type because the open-ended question type creates friction for people to answer and might sometimes be difficult to understand and interpret.

Heuristic Evaluations

Since you now have a working prototype, a heuristic evaluation, otherwise known as usability review will serve as a low cost method which can be used for checking your initial product iteration against usability best practices. The heuristic evaluation can also provide you with a workable system for competitive benchmarking since you can compare competitors against the same criteria. The heuristics review, though cheap and requires only one or two days, cannot precisely tell you the system's usability. This is because you are not testing against real users of the product. The heuristics reviews are also subjected to inconsistency and subjectivity since they are reviews from different people with different preferences. Consider the scenario based approach below to guide you;

• Define your usability review scenarios — Define important and common users' tasks. Who are the ones using the product and consider if that is their first time using the product. What is the specific task they are trying to carry out with the product and what result are they expecting to get within a particular time? For instance, when evaluating a phone product, you would consider some scenarios such as making calls and sending messages.

• Walk the talk — Now that you have been able to define each scenario, you will need to walk through the steps one after the other to achieve user goals. Can users get to know how to use this product? How will they know if they are doing the correct thing? Walk through each scenario yourself and consider yourself as a user. Do this till you are sure you achieve your end goal with your product. If you can (as a user), they most probably can too.

• Design a heuristic review scorecard and have it completed — Design a template to serve as your checklist. You can design a 40-point checklist and have about three to five people from your team do the same thing. Be reminded that a high product score point doesn't necessarily translate that your product or application is usable, but it does mean that it might be acceptable by a wide range of users.

User Research Report

Having checked your prototype or product against all best practices, it is now time to verify your findings by adopting real users. Methods like tree testing, moderated user testing, un-moderated user testing and card sorting can all be deployed.

While usability testing can actually be more expensive than any heuristic evaluations you can carry out, but since you need

to plan and opt for controlled experiments, there might be no other better way to confirm how your product or application might perform in the market. But conducting a proper market research will lead you to understand what users do and even when they do the things they do. You can then utilize user research to fill in the other gaps and to answer why they do what they do. To get a good grasp of what users do and how they do it, you can consider the five (5) frameworks below;

• Objectives — design framing questions such as Who would watch TV shows? Why would they watch TV shows? You can then give priority to the most important questions, and translate those questions into better and focus objectives such as "Determine how frequent people watch TV shows in America?" share video clips?"

• Hypotheses — By using your framing questions, you can spend about 8 minutes individually scheming. You might be able to come up with attitudinal hypotheses (TV shows watchers in the United States love to know their relative's favorite TV shows), feature specific hypothesis (TV shows watchers in the United States only share shows if they are well known shows with others), or behavioral hypothesis (TV shows watchers in the United States only tell their relatives about TV shows they find interesting).

• Methods — Sort all your collected hypotheses based on their themes (features/attitude/behavior) and you can now assign your testing tactics. For instance, contextual and observational interviews are good ways for getting to learn things. You can navigate more design ideas by using paper prototyping, diary studies and many other collaborative actions.

• Conduct — Recruit around ten (10) different users for four (4) testing sessions each (about 1-hour duration). Come with your own interview guide and then properly all the photos, notes and videos of people you test. Reaffirm your objectives by constantly asking yourself if you are actually getting what you are required to learn to achieve your desired objective. If you are not getting what you need, then you can change tactics.

• Synthesize — The reason behind the data you collected is actually very important. Is there a system that suggests that you will need new project design? Did the things you have learnt teach more tactics of how to change your design and research objective? And will you even need to modify the design actions that you have previously planned? You can check the list of Do's and Don'ts for usability testing below;

- Endeavor to involve yourself in all activities that can ensure the success of the product and also observe testing as much as possible. You should not conclude on the design just with a few usability tests.

- You should avoid using the testing period for product demonstration. It is not a product demonstration, it is called a testing session for a reason.

When you are in the field testing your new features or products, you can employ the service of someone to help you make a video record of the reactions of the consumers while seeing the product or learning about the product.

Analytics Reports

Analytics reports are just a quantitative addition to the mostly qualitative processes you have been seeing so far. It cannot be argued that qualitative approaches such as heuristic reviews and user research are bottom-up methods of analyzing end-users, it is as well not debatable that analytics methods provide a top-down approach because you are converting a wide range of data from users into a few insights. Analytics possess traditionally recognized marketing strategy but it is still widely used and acceptable in user research and design. Since qualitative research is somewhat expensive, you can actually obtain a bird-eye view of potential testing scenarios and issues based on analytics reports.

For user research, report analytics serves 3 important roles for recognizing new tests and then validating existing tests:

• Indicating issues — You can design weekly metrics reports to diagnose issues in applications or products that are web based. For instance, let us say you recently redesign your WordPress website and added new features. You might notice after two weeks that either the visitors are constant on the website or the number of visitors dropped or the number of visitors actually increase. The metrics can successfully predict the increase or decrease in the number of visitors either per week or per month depending on how you want it.

• Investigating issues —If any issues are flagged, you can investigate further. Is the decrease in conversions coming from a specific device? If so, you could design a device-specific A/B user test to check possible solutions.

• Verifying qualitative research — Report analytics can as well helps you identify trouble areas that come up during user testing. For example, let us say during the usability testing, some participants were unable to find contents on your website simply because you use an ambiguous word, which seems confusing. You can deploy a tool like Google Analytics to examine the keyword traffic for those words. If the analytics show a large volume, then you will be rest assured that the problem is solvable.

If your interest lies in specific user segments, then you can also deploy cohort analysis to know what further testing and research you can do. For instance, if you have an online shop, you can consider customers who patronize your store on Tuesday as a cohort, do a behavioral analysis and design user testing for as appropriate.

If you do not have a working product yet, analytics are still okay for conducting market research. You can deploy a tool such as Google Adwords to look for search volumes and infer consumers' interest and also competition. You can also use the backlink analysis to understand if your competitors are advertising similar products that you have.

Research, Test and Validate

When you conduct a market research, you will be able to see the broad concept of what a wide range of people will likely go for when shopping for a product. But a user research properly conducted will enable you to tailor your production technique to meet individual taste while not compromising the values you obtained by conducting the market research. Essentially, user research enables you to see things that are immediately practicable. Both the market research and the tailored user research have a big role to play in your products' overall development and success. When you integrate user research with market research, you get a way to hear from the market as well as the users of the products you are creating. With that in place, you proceed to design solutions that actually work. Your raw research is still useful as it begins to assume shapes and forms during the product's analysis stage.

CHAPTER THREE

ANALYZING USERS BEFORE THE DESIGN STAGE

While you might understand what product you want to create, it would be difficult to have a good product experience without getting to understand the end-users first. Needless is to say that the best product experience you can have begins with knowing your end-users. Knowing their names, the jobs they do or how many kids they have are not just enough. You need to comprehend them to the point that will make you understand their fears, motivations, behaviors and mentality. That does not necessarily translate that you will need to pack in and start living them. No, that is not the point we are making here. This guide will teach how you can get to know your users and understand them at the basic level. The right question you probably have in your mind right now is "how then can we get to know our users if we are not going to live with them"? Once you have understood what your product is all about (product's definition) and how the product will address the needs of the people (current market), you can now begin to get started on your way to understanding your end-users. Getting to understand your users will go a long way to determine whether users will like your product or not. Your aim, in this case, is to comprehend their struggles, and then measure their reactions to your products.

Why Analysis is Important

User analysis provides answers to your questions concerning end users goals and tasks so that these results can enable you to make the right decisions concerning development and design. Specifically, you will be able to notice roles and specify characteristics or features that are not, in fact, always possible through market research such as state of mind, knowledge, use cases and environment, comfort with similar products and usage frequency. These insights ensure that feature changes only rely on data from consumers who will pay for the product versus the opinions of stakeholders who are ready to move the product processes forward. A thorough user analysis allows more profitable product domination in the market. This is because user analysis enables product consumers to decide your product's path, and the knowledge you garnered can help reduce time wastage when it comes to heavy decision making.

When you enter a dilemma owing to conflicting opinions and views, user analysis allows you to navigate in the proper direction based on facts that are concrete. Check below some special benefits of user analysis;

• Better and improved products — Processes that take end users into consideration as well as those processes that understand business motives and objectives will always give rise to products that work well for the purpose for which they are intended for.

• Cheaper to fix problems — User analysis enables you to match up your product and compare it against reality to make allowable changes while it is still exactly just on paper. It is cheaper to fix an error in your product while it is in prototype stage than to fix any small thing in the live product.

• Ease of use is an agreed upon requirement — You must have seen consumers using the term "usability" and "user experience" as often as possible when talking about features they desire most in a product. Everybody wants to use a product that can give them maximum satisfaction, even if they have to pay more. This is one of the reasons why you see people going for premium software that cost more online than the free packages. Essentially, user analysis brings your products or applications to a point where it will have a better selling point.

Personas

While it may look almost difficult to create a person out of nothing, building a persona is a very important step to understanding the psychology of your potential customers.

Personas serve to concentrate product decisions by including some elements of real-world scenarios to the equation. They behave almost like another guy in the room when you are in the process of making important product decisions. However, personas should not address all your product's needs nor represent all audiences, but should rather concentrate on the main needs of the most relevant user groups. It is important to understand that you cannot satisfy everyone with your product as this is a quick way to lose. This is why it is important to recognize your targeted audiences and tailor your product to meet their specific needs. There are products meant for the bourgeoisie class of the economy and there will equally be products meant for the lower class. If your product is meant for the former, there is no reason why you should be targeting the latter unless you are thinking of expanding your market capability. Essentially, building a persona allows you to integrate potential customers and deal with them like you would deal with a real human. You can work with three to five personals as this is big enough to cut across most user groups, but it is still not enough to have a precise opinion of consumers' psychology. You can check the information you can consider to record while working with a personal;

• Give the persona a name — You can give the person whatever name you desire, but you need to make the name a real one so that the person will feel like a real human being who want to buy your product.

• Identify the job, role, and company — You can utilize surveys to cover this kind of information.

• Include necessary information — While gender, age, and device usage might be necessary, you can as well do well by describing the user's psychology. Enumerate their expectations, aspirations and fears. You can deploy some metric tools for demographics and insightful guesses for psychographics. It is necessary to point that basic personas most times don't feature all the details that drive consumers' purchases. But you can use interviews and psychology of consumers to morph personals into behaviors that are otherwise analyzable when it comes to consumers' experience, fears and motivations. As you consider creating your personals, you can do some reality checks by carrying out a segmental interview. This way, you can be able to integrate real data inside your personals by interviewing your existing consumers, referrals and prospects.

User Stories & Job Stories

Once you have some clear insights of who your product's users are likely to be, you can then begin to analyze and map out how they are likely to utilize the product you have created. This enables improved product design. You can consider the following guides as a tip when developing your user stories;

• Independent — The user story should be one that is self-contained to ensure that it is independent of other stories.

• Negotiable — Avoid putting too much personal detail so that the user stories can be flexible and can be modified at will.

• Valuable — Your user stories must be one that can give values to the intended end-users.

• Estimable — You must be able to estimate and quantify the resources you would need for a user story

• Scalable — Make the user stories lightweight so that the stories can be tasked and assign priority with a definite amount of certainty.

• Testable — Provide the story's acceptance criteria so that the team can know when the story is complete.

A complete user story must be one that provides clarity about the type of consumer you are talking about, describe the actions carried out with details and provide adequate clarity on the context in which the actions must be carried out. Job stories are actually more actionable because they concentrate on motivation rather than implementation.

Defining Your Vision

While use cases examine how your personas might use your product, the experience map actually takes a much advanced level view of the user as part of a defined product's journey helping you to better modify your product to pass the true usability test.

Know your Users

If your product is not designed for users, then it is only designed for no one or probably it is designed for you. Consumers or product users don't really care if the advert says your product can carry out a million and one tasks. All that they need is your product to solve their own problem. Understanding this basic thing will enable you to create products that are user-friendly. You have to understand your users as a person and get to know why they need the product they need.

CHAPTER FOUR

THE RULE OF SEVEN: FACTORS THAT INFLUENCE USER EXPERIENCE

Before you dive into the full product design processes, it is essential that you consider the seven (7) factors that influence user experience. It is no more news that User Experience (UX) is important when discussing the failure or success of your product in the market. UX is often misrepresented with usability which is a function of how easy it is to utilize a particular product. While it might be true that you cannot think of UX without thinking about product usability, UX has morphed beyond that as it has evolved to integrate much more user psychology than the usability level. It therefore becomes imperative that you explore deeper into the psychology of users before you can be able to get a full understanding of the market platform. The seven factors that influence users' experience include;

- *Useful*
- *Usable*
- *Findable*
- *Credible*
- *Desirable*
- *Accessible*

- *Valuable*

Let us try to see how each of these factors influences users' experience;

1. Useful

Your product's importance lies in its usefulness. If your product is not useful (serves no need), do you think users will like to invest their money on it? If your product serves no purpose, it is not likely to survive in a market full of other useful products. Just as beauty is in the hands of the beholder, the same thing applies to a product's usefulness. The product you deem useful might not be useful to another user. For instance, a 4 years old kid will probably find a baby toy useful while an adult might not find such a product useful. Likewise, the fact that a product is not one that users can use to generate money doesn't make it useless. We all individual needs and a product don't necessarily have to be bringing money for you before it can be considered useful. Thus, if a product gives non-practical or monetary benefit it might still be useful depending on who is using such a product. This is the reason why you should try and familiarize yourself with most or all of the tips given in the previous chapters to ensure that you take users into consideration while building your product.

2. Usable

Usability has to do with allowing users to achieve their end goals with a product as much as they want without difficulty. Let us, for instance, assume that you are a video game developer and you then develop a video game with five consoles or pads, your game might not be essentially usable. This is because, at least normal people, do not have more than two hands. Your products might still record huge success if they are not usable; this is because the first buyers might be so many that they do not get to know in time that the product is not that applicable. Poor usability is most often linked with debut products – think the first generation of TV sets most of which are no longer applicable in this century. To avoid a worse scenario, always endeavor to create a product that users will find usable.

3. Findable

Of what use is your product if it cannot be easily tracked in the market? Findable refers to the notion that your product must be very easy to find, and in the world of digital and information materials, the content inside your product must be easy to locate too. Let us, for instance, say you uploaded your digital book (eBook), and the book is not arranged for proper content indexing, do you think people will still read? The reason is not far fetched: people hate stress and they most probably will go for things which stress them less. If you are browsing an educational website and you are finding it tough to locate the content that you need, you would most likely consider visiting another website. If you are reading a newspaper and all the contents and stories within the paper were inserted at random pages anyhow, instead of sectionalizing those pages into categories such as entertainment, sports, business, economy etc., you would easily get bored within little time and won't even consider reading such paper going forward. Time is of essence to all humans because we have limited time to spend in life. People want to come to your online store, shop for the goods they want, pay for the service and jet out as soon as possible. You can now see why most people won't have time navigating your website if the contents you put there are not even findable to begin with. Ability to find your product within a small time, thus, is essential for a unique user experience.

4. Credible

The 21st century buyers don't have time as you have seen in the previous concept. Nobody will give you a second chance to deceive them twice. This is because there are multitudes of credible sellers who are offering the same service just like yours. If your products are not credible, buyers will run in a matter of seconds should you not give them another reason to stay. When we say credibility, we are referring to the ability of the user to have trust in the service you provide. Have you ever seen a situation where people won't buy a product anywhere else if their regular supplier is not available? That is credibility for short. They have ultimate trust in the product of their regular supplier and they are not ready to compromise that for anything; they would rather wait. When your product does the exact same actions you say it will do, and lasts for the same amount of time you indicated; then it is fit and has passed the credibility test. It becomes almost impossible for you to deliver a unique product user experience if your buyers think you are a serial liar and are not supposed to be trusted with anything. Another reason why you should always strive to leave the impression with your products is that consumers are more likely to tell others of their bad experience with your product which is not even a good sign. They most likely would not want their friends or relatives to fall victim of the same product.

5. Desirable

Let us, for example, consider two car products. One is elegant, shows class and taste and is very attractive. The other one is not so attractive and cannot make heads turn twice. Which one do you think will be most desirable by buyers? Your guess is as good as mine. Desirability is often pronounced in a product when you look at its design, aesthetic (beauty), branding, image and emotional design. The more desirable you think your gadget is, the more you flaunt it to ignite desire in the mind of other people. This is envy, if you see it that way too. A product that shouts "hey, look at me" is most often desired.

6. Accessible

Is your product accessible? If you want to answer this question appropriately, your product must be one that is reachable by all, not excluding any part of the demographics. Unfortunately, business owners or creators sometimes confuse a product's accessibility with the ability to find a product. When you are considering your product's accessibility, you should be looking at whether you are able to provide that unique experience which is accessible by users having a wide range of abilities – this features those with one or two disabilities such as vision, walking, hearing or learning disability. Designing products for accessibility is often perceived as waste of time and resources by most companies. This is because they are of the opinion that people with disabilities only make up a small segment of the population. This is not always true. In fact, the statistics of disable people in the United States is about 21%; and it will probably be higher than this in most developing and underdeveloped nations of the world. If your product domiciled in the United States, this statistics will imply that one out of five people will not have access to your product if you don't tailor your product to meet the needs of people with disabilities. It is worthy to reiterate that when you design for accessibility, you will see that you are making a product which is usable by everyone, and not just people with disabilities. You cannot underemphasize the importance of accessibility in user design. In addition, accessible product design has now become a legal obligation in some parts of the world, such as the European Union. Failure to deliver accessibility in your designs may lead to fines. Unfortunately, this legal obligation is not being enforced much as it should. Nonetheless, there can always be an improvement going forward.

7. Valuable

Lastly, your product must be able to deliver value. It must be able to deliver value to the business which builds it and as well to the user who purchases it or uses it. Without your product providing the right value, it is possible that any prior success of the product will later wane as the truth of natural economics begins to undermine it. As designers, you should have it in your mind that value is one of the key influences to make decisions on purchases. A $200 product that is able to solve a $20,000 problem is one that is likely to succeed; a $20,000 product that solves a $200 problem is far less likely to succeed.

CHAPTER FIVE

ABRIEF INSIGHT INTO PRODUCT'S USABILITY

Many people usually confuse usability with user experience (UX). The fact is that usability is not the same thing as User experience (UX). The usability of a particular product is an important factor that determines and furnishes its user experience; hence usability falls under user experience. To many people, usability is all about the ease at which a particular product can be used; it is, of course, more than that. Usability can be referred to as the extent to which a particular product can be utilized by users to accomplish specific goals, with efficiency, effectiveness, and satisfaction in a specified usage context. Hence, usability is more than just how users can carry out tasks with ease. Usability, though, is concerned with user contentment. Look at it from this perspective, for a website to be actually effective and usable, it must be engaging to you and of course serves usability, coupled with good appearance.

Before we go further into what usability really means, talking about the importance of usability is crucial. Usability matters because if the end-users are not able to achieve their goals effectively, efficiently, and in a reasonable manner, they are prone to seeking an alternative remedy to satisfy their needs.

And that might mean they won't patronize your product or website anymore.

Moreover, for applications and websites, alternative remedies are too much available at every door step which makes them easy to explore. Simply put, if your product's usability is not top-notch, its user experience won't be a good one, and consumers most probably will leave your products for another. As product makers planning to create products that can last the test of time, it is expedient to make sure that your products are actually usable for users; otherwise you might be losing interesting buyers. Web user analysis revealed that more than 44% of users leave a website simply because they don't understand what the company or the website is all about (ineffective messaging platform), a little over 42% leave websites owing to absence of contact information on the website, and above 35% of users leave owing to poor website design or navigation. This web user analysis is actually telling you the harm which poor usability can cause to your website or products. Usability essentially refers to as the result of a user-oriented design process. That is a process that tries to check how and why a consumer will choose a product and then hopes to evaluate that use. That process is an iterative process and hopes to improve with each continuous evaluation cycle.

The five (5) characteristics of a usable product

The following criteria are the five criteria which your product must meet before it can be considered usable;

- **Effectiveness**
- **Efficiency**
- **Engagement**
- **Error tolerance**
- **Ease of learning**

Effectiveness

Effectiveness talks about whether product users can achieve their goals with a high level of accuracy. Much of a product's effectiveness actually originates from the level of supports given to the product users when they use the product. For instance, let us say you design an ecommerce website, and you make your payment platform such that it only takes a valid credit card digit. This will go a long way towards reducing data entry error and allow your visitors or buyers to do their jobs with less difficulty. There are many means by which you can get your buyers to do their task as correctly as possible; the key lies in giving adequate information to help them navigate your product without necessarily seeking help.

You should also try and refine the language and tone you used in your products. The less ambiguous the language and the tone is, the more easy it is for the information you are trying to pass across to have the best impact on people you are communicating with. This doesn't necessarily translate that you should reduce your language totally; it does mean that you should use the right language style with simplicity so that your buyers can understand you. You might also consider using the right technical terms; say for example, you can cut down on the amount of technical coding terms for your website.

If in doubt of anything, endeavor always to keep it direct and simple; unless of course you are actually selling a ghost-writing service, you are not likely to attract customers with high-level prose. Redundancy in navigation can, at times, be useful; if users have multiple routes to reach their objective, they are more likely to find their way there. However, this may very much reduce the overall workability of the process. So, you should always think of the frustration of your end-users who might be finding it difficult to navigate your product and move forward.

Efficiency

Effectiveness and efficiency have come to be not too direct in the mind. However, they are quite different from a usability perspective. Efficiency tries to focus on speed. Efficiency essentially considers how fast the users are likely to get the job done.

You might probably want to check the number of steps (or indeed clicks/keystrokes) you will need to achieve the objective; can they be reduced? This will enable you to develop efficient processes. When you design your website with vividly labeled navigation buttons with clear uses, you will be able to provide users with clear website functions and they will be happier visiting your website.

30

The deployment of meaningful shortcuts (for instance, consider the number of hours you have saved using Ctrl+C and Ctrl+V to copy and paste any text on your computer) on your website will also help you to develop and maximize efficient processes.

In another sense, to improve efficiency, you need to consider how your consumers prefer to access your products or website—are they visiting your website via their smartphones or their desktop computer with a big keyboard and mouse? The two gadgets need very different methods of navigation.

Engagement

Engagement might be a flesh of a buzzword, but if you can see through the bone, you will see that engagement happens when the consumers find the product nice and gratifying to utilize. Aesthetics count here, and it is the main reason why many companies invest a small part of their budget in graphic design elements—but aesthetics are not even the only determining factor when we are talking about engagement. Engagement is not only about the product looking nice but also explores more about the product seeming right. If you are creating beautiful products that lack content, you can't expect users to be satisfied. Essentially, beauty matters but it is the satisfaction users are planning to derive from your product that matter most. Proper layouts, readable typography and website's ease of navigation all feature together to bring the right interaction for your users and make the product engaging. Looking nice is not everything.

Error tolerance

It looks almost impossible that, given the desire to have any degree of sophistication or complexity, you can totally remove errors in your products; most especially, digital products may be more prone to error due to the environment in which they find themselves; an environment which, sometimes, is beyond the control of the developers or the users themselves. Nonetheless, it is actually important that you should be able to reduce the errors from occurring and to make sure that, even if the error does occur, your users are able to get back on track almost immediately. This is the principle behind error tolerance. Consider the tips below if you are determined to promote error tolerance;

- Restricting opportunities to carry out a wrong action on your website or application. Endeavor to make buttons or links as clear and distinct as possible; keep tones and languages simple and clear; avoid using jargons unless it is absolutely necessary and try to keep dependencies in actions or forms together. You should also try to reduce or eliminate options to correct or erase choices as much as possible, and try to provide guides and samples when requesting users to input data.

- Provide the chance to 'redo'. Provide users a method to reconfigure and re-enter what they have just input and go back to start again. In the same vein, give a clearly accessible 'undo' function. Consider the amount of data a user can stand to lose if he/she mistakenly deleted an item. The idea that their data or information can still be recovered even if they mistakenly press a wrong item will keep users safe from panicking.

- Assuming people are going to do things you are not expecting them to do. Offer to help by offering advice or support on how to get them back on track. This simple recovery support goes a long way to show users that you are humane and believe humanity. All of these highlighted recovery methods also let your website look more human and worthy to be trusted. It also shows that you understand how and why human beings can make mistakes and you are ready to support them to make sense of what they think they might have lost.

Ease of learning

If you want your product or website to be used as often as possible, then you need users to be able to learn and understand their steps around it; to the point that it comes as a mere walk in the pack when they use such a product again. You also need to provide a space for ease of learning when you want to release new features and functionality; otherwise, a loyal and consistent user may easily get frustrated and angry with your new release. This is a normal trend on most of the social network platforms; whenever a product manufacturer releases a new and updated set of functionality and features, they are always welcomed with a lot of outbursts from users who have liked the previous versions and are finding it difficult navigating the new version. This is most of the time a worrying scenario even when the new functions are not exactly hard to comprehend or navigate; users will still complain.

The best method to support ease of learning is by designing systems that match a user's formal mental models. A mental model is literally a representation of a particular thing in the actual world and how it is done from the perspective of the user. It is why virtual buttons will look much like real buttons – we understand that we press buttons; therefore, we click virtual buttons on phones with touch screens or mouse-click the phones. The form ignites the appropriate scenario in the user, hence making such things very easy to learn.

Usability + utility = usefulness

When you are designing a product for usability, trying to think about utility is crucial, too. While usability is more concerned about making functions very easy and welcoming to use, utility is all about creating functions that users need, to begin with. A product becomes more useful to users when you relate usability with utility.

A mobile payment application, for instance, could give the most usable functionality of adding the people near you on Facebook; nonetheless, because most users of that app would not be needing that feature, it is going to, probably, be useless to them. All of the efforts and resources you have invested towards creating the most user-friendly features and functionality could go to waste if that feature won't be needed anyways. It is pointless creating a feature users don't need.

CHAPTER SIX

RESEARCH TECHNIQUES USED BY USER EXPERIENCE DESIGNERS

The following research techniques can be used by UX designers;

1. Card Sorting

Card sorting has been in existence since ages, even long before the idea of UX design. It involves writing phrases or words on some pieces of cards and asking the users to categorize them. You can even ask the users to label the categories of cards they have sorted. The words or phrases that you have written on the card actually depend on what you want to find out from the users. For example, if you are trying to find out whether the Information Architecture on your website, or the way your website information is arranged, is simple to understand, you can write the different sections or pages of your website on the card and then ask a user to sort the cards into categories. If, on the other hand, you are only interested to know how users think about financial planning, you can write down different activities on the card ("invest in Forex market "travel once every two years", "applying for jobs in other part of the world", etc.) and then tell your users to sort them by priority. There are various types of card-sorting methods, and picking the right one is crucial. Better still, there are many online tools that will enable you to do card sorting remotely, enabling you to leverage the technique locally and globally.

Advantages of card sorting

- It is a less expensive user research method, since face to face online software may be quite expensive.
- It is also a quite simple method for users to comprehend and understand.
- It is a very simple way of getting users' input (or even to collect user validation) for useful ideas early on in a UX design project.
- It requires little to zero effort at all to prepare a card-sorting technique.

2. Expert Review

Expert reviews entails a single 'professional' navigating through a product or website through the User Interface (UI) and checking for issues with the design result, accessibility, and product's usability. There are no ground processes to follow, and the techniques or methodologies of the expert review might vary from professional to professional and also from product to product. The more experienced the reviewer has in product usability and UX design, the more useful the input of that reviewer will be (in most cases).

Advantages of the Expert review

- It is quick, cheap and easy. This is exactly the case when you compare this method to more formal usability-testing techniques.
- It only requires a single expert to carry out an expert review. This will diagnose most of the things that might have gone wrong during the design stage.
- It is a good way to inform more UX research; however, you need to be careful when conducting an expert review at face value—you should not allow it to preclude further user testing; rather, dig deeper and check how you can get more thorough and useful insights.

3. Eye movement tracking

Knowing where your product users are looking when they are using your product or application can let you know a great deal concerning where your design's effectiveness lies. Eye movement tracking can help with UI design, and it allows you to know how to give priority to some particular type of content. This technique method was created for academic research. The method is also used extensively in medical research, and it has become very popular and cost-effective worthy to be incorporated by UX designers, too.

Advantages of eye tracking techniques

- Given the ever-improving state of the art in technology, the advancements have long since left bulky and invasive eye movement tracking systems behind. Consequently, eye movement tracking has become so sophisticated and discreet that modern systems do not interfere with the results of usability tests.
- Hand in hand with those developments, the technology has become increasingly affordable. Eye movement tracking may not be applicable to all projects, but it will not make you spend too much either.
- The technology has become so profound now, more than ever before, that reliable results can now be obtained within a reasonable amount of time. It is sufficient to say that the result obtained from this technique has been tried and tested by UX designers and has been shown to be reliable.
- UX design clients enjoy the eye movement tracking method. It is really a good way to show why they might decide to invest in further usability testing.

4. Field study

The UX researchers might divide themselves in groups, go out and observe product users in actions while using the product. This way, they can measure a certain behavioral index of users consuming the product. This method is good since it involves live actions where researchers get to interact with product users. They might even decide to ask the users some questions about how they are enjoying the product under certain contexts. Field studies, most times, feature interviews, observations, contextual enquiry and ethnographic research.

Advantages of Field studies technique

- There is no better form of research other than getting to see users behaving as they will behave when they utilize your product. Researchers admire these techniques and they are often interested in persuading clients to bring them on board.
- When done very well, the results of field studies give the deepest analysis into user problems and fears, and provide clearer pathways towards feasible solutions.

5. Usability testing

Usability testing has become the face of UX research and has been deployed by many firms who consider it a feasible means of getting to know their product's feedback. Usability testing essentially involves users carrying out a specific task with the product or application. Such usability testing can concentrate on a single process, or better still can be wider in range of processes.

Advantages of usability testing

- There is probably no greater method to comprehend what consumers do with the product than actually looking at them doing things with the product. The only constraint is that it might not work well if you don't select the right users for the test.
- Usability tests give specific results which often results in specific actions. Better still, it is very difficult for people to go against decisions based on these tests; it is, in fact, nearly impossible to go against evidence of user behavior.
- You can incorporate clients into usability testing just as easily as you would an observer. This boosts their enthusiasm for such testing and depicts visibly why such testing adds value.

CHAPTER SEVEN

THINGS TO CONSIDER WHEN DESIGNING USER EXPERIENCE FOR MOBILE

If you want to design for mobile, there are lots of things you are required to consider. You have to take into consideration the way that the device is used and the features that make up the mobile itself. There are some guiding principles that can guide you to start designing for mobile, but you should not forget that these guides cannot replace the user research. Aside from the standard UX design considerations, there are also some mobile-specific design factors. For example, are you going to incorporate your mobile offering together with your current offering? Will you be deploying responsive design or you will use adaptive design?

A lot of these questions will be anchored to context—that is, the context in which phone users are likely to use their mobile gadgets to do whatever things they have in mind. If your product or app users access the mobile web using their desks, that is good, but many users do not access their mobile website using their desk to anchor their mobile devices. They are most probably going to be trying to utilize their mobile devices in the mall, market, busy places, on their commute to work or to the coffee shop etc.

Space (where users will be using their mobile gadgets) and occasion (i.e., context) should be primal in your mind. As the advent of civilization and technology has freed almost everyone from having to restrain themselves to desks just to get online, the places in which they use their mobile gadgets now are almost uncountable. This implies that you will have to factor in how to limit distractions and make it especially easy for the mobile users to concentrate on the job in their hands.

Basic design considerations for mobile web

1. Small screens

You cannot obviously compare the screen resolution or size for mobile gadgets with that of personal computers and laptops. The screen size for PCs is far larger than that of mobile. While designing for mobile, you will be considering making designs for more than one screen size; this is because the screen size of phones varies from device to device. You can decide to adopt the responsive design method (where the mobile device will be able to automatically handle the change in display itself) or adaptive design (where the server takes care of the change). You might start from a "mobile first" method where you will be designing for the smallest of mobile phones in the market, and then building it up from there.

2. Keep navigation simple and straightforward

- Prioritize navigation according to the way users use functionality—the most popular should be at the top.
- Reduce the amounts of navigation involved
- Ensure the navigation labelling is clear and concise for easy navigation
- Provide short-key functionality for easy access to different features.

3. Keep content to a minimum

- Make sure that your contents will be supported on every device.
- Don't bore your users with too much content.

4. Minimize the input required from users

- Keep the website address as short as possible.

About Author

*M*aurice Jayson is a prolific UX designer who has worked for more than 12 years of his career as a UX designer. He understands UX design so perfectly that he has many online for where he teaches UX design for free. Maurice is happily married with two children.

www.ingramcontent.com/pod-product-compliance
Lightning Source LLC
LaVergne TN
LVHW051604050326
832903LV00033B/4364

* 9 7 9 8 6 7 5 9 6 4 9 0 1 *